Reading Roundabout

What I Like to Eat

Paul Humphrey

Photography by Chris Fairclough

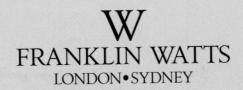

W
FRANKLIN WATTS
LONDON·SYDNEY

First published in 2005 by
Franklin Watts
96 Leonard Street
London EC2A 4XD

Franklin Watts Australia
Level 17/207 Kent Street
Sydney NSW 2000

ISBN 0 7496 6182 8 (hbk)
ISBN 0 7496 6194 1 (pbk)

Dewey classification number: 641.3

A CIP catalogue record for this book is available
from the British Library.

Planning and production by Discovery Books Limited
Editor: Rachel Tisdale
Designer: Ian Winton
Photography: Chris Fairclough
Series advisors: Diana Bentley MA and Dee Reid MA,
Fellows of Oxford Brookes University

The author, packager and publisher would like to thank the following people
for their participation in this book: Megan Merten-Jones and family, Mr Skellen
and the pupils of St Peter's Primary School, Harborne.

Printed in China

Contents

I like eating toast for breakfast.

My brother
likes cereal.

I like eating a crunchy apple at break time.

Our packed lunches
have lots of
nice things to
eat in them.

9

After school, I have a biscuit and a drink.

11

For dinner, I like
slurpy soup.
My brother
likes it too.

13

I like my mum's curries ...

... but my brother doesn't.

We both like
my dad's roast
chicken.

We both love eating ice cream.

19

Sometimes, Mum buys us a chocolate bar to share.

Guess what food we like best?

Party food!

Word bank

Look back for these words and pictures.

Apple

Biscuit

Cereal

Chicken

Chocolate

Drink

Ice cream

Soup

Toast